BOOK TWO

POTTAG-HOVEY METHOD

for

FRENCH HORN

by

MAX. P. POTTAG

and

NILO W. HOVEY

A LOGICAL VOLUME II to the famous "POTTAG-HOVEY METHOD - BOOK I"
or any other good elementary instructor

ED. LIBR.
No. 106

Made in U.S.A.

FOREWORD

A worthy student of the French Horn must strive constantly for a finer quality of tone, a wider range, greater technical facility and more intelligent phrasing. The player whose previous efforts have qualified him for the study of a more advanced method has likely come to this realization and it is with these needs in mind that the material was selected for Book II of the Pottag-Hovey Method for French Horn.

The daily practice of sustained tones is essential in the development of quality and for this purpose the scale studies are recommended. The slow etudes are included for tone development and for phrasing studies as well. Rapid tonguing, increased technique in fingering and intelligent use of the legato, marcato and staccato styles may be taken up in connection with the scale and chord studies.

Development of the upper and lower registers of the instrument is too often neglected, in fact, it might be added that the study of these notes is often dismissed with the excuse that they are impractical, impossible, or both. This may be partly due to the fact that the Horn parts of elementary Band and Orchestra music seldom require more than a reasonable command of the notes in the staff. While this is justifiable, the fact must not be overlooked that the finest solo and ensemble literature as well as the moderate to difficult grades of Band and Orchestra music require a much wider range.

For most students, the material may be taken up in the order in which it is presented. Detailed study of each exercise and etude with the aim of a perfect reading will be of greatest value, while a superficial playing of the same material will be of practically no benefit. MAKE ACCURACY A HABIT.

A Lesson In Proper Interpretation

One of the most common faults of amateur musicians is the failure to adjust *note values* to fit the character and tempo of the composition being played. If the student is to develop any semblance of style and if his music is to be expressive in any degree, this important phase of musicianship must be given careful consideration.

There is no foundation for the idea that proper interpretation cannot be taught and that definite rules dealing with the subject of note values cannot be established. Exceptions to such rules can be found, but the performer who has been thoroughly drilled on the subject will find his knowledge an asset in intelligent music reading.

The habit of playing with acceptable style can be firmly established if the following suggestions are applied to the simplest of exercises, including the scale and chord studies which are contained in this book.

written:
1
played:

The notes must be very broad and sustained. A good example is this passage from "Stradella:"

Horn in D
Horn in F

Do not "cheat" the short notes in value and do not play them softer. All short notes must be played as loud as the others unless marked otherwise.

written:
2
played:

The notes should be gracefully "lifted." A good example is a passage from the 3rd movement of Brahms 2nd symphony.

written:
played:

The notes should be staccato. The example is from the Scherzo of Beethoven's 5th Symphony:

The notes should be gracefully "lifted." The example is from "Shepherds Dance," from "Henry VIII" by German:

In Scotch music the dotted note is a little more sustained.

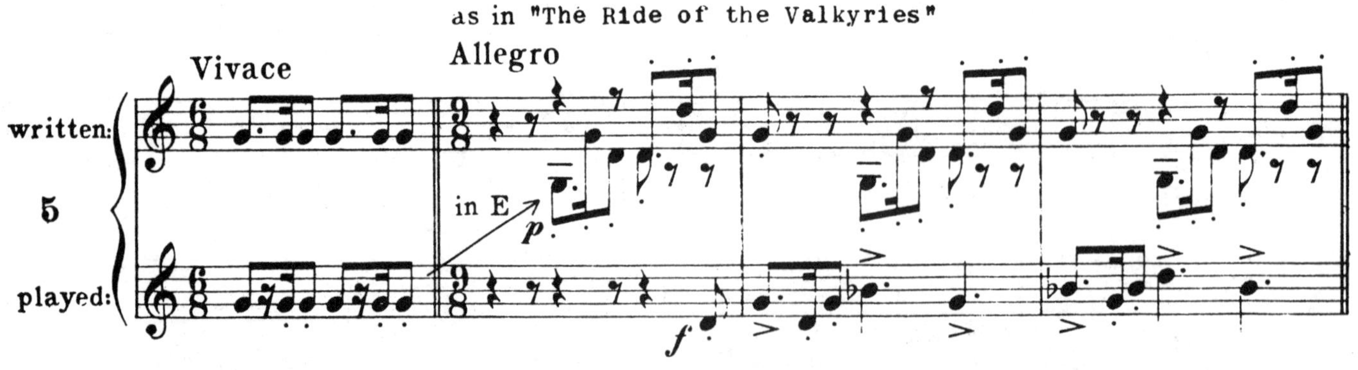

As a test of the student's ability to adjust values properly, the following simple melody should be played in three tempo markings — Adagio, Allegretto, Alla Breve.

Note the difference in value of the 3rd and 4th quarters in measures 1-3-5&7, when played to the three tempo markings as given above.

Scale and Chord Patterns

All scales and chords appearing in this book should be practiced according to the various patterns given below in C Major. In addition to the detached half, quarter, eighth and sixteenth notes, it is important for the sake of flexibility that ALL SCALES AND CHORDS BE PRACTICED SLURRED. All scales and chords should be memorized.

Note: Play all scale exercises written in half notes in a broad style, but with a good clean attack.

Do not neglect to practice all the previous scales & chords "slurred".

A Tone Study

All "Tone Studies" should be practiced as slowly as possible, for tone development, soft tonguing, phrasing & breath control.

Adagio

16

Etude

Andantino

17

A Staccato Exercise

Allegro

18

It is advisable to practice all scales in one octave at first, especially the Minor scales, to establish the difference between Major and Minor.

The A Minor scale (harmonic form)

19
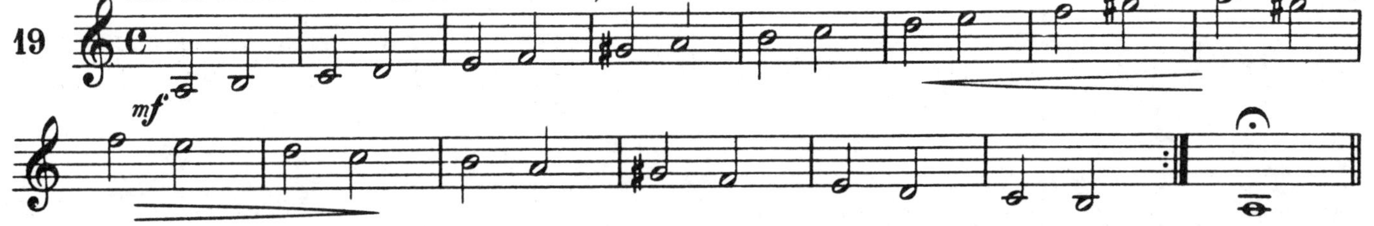

The A Minor scale (melodic form)

20
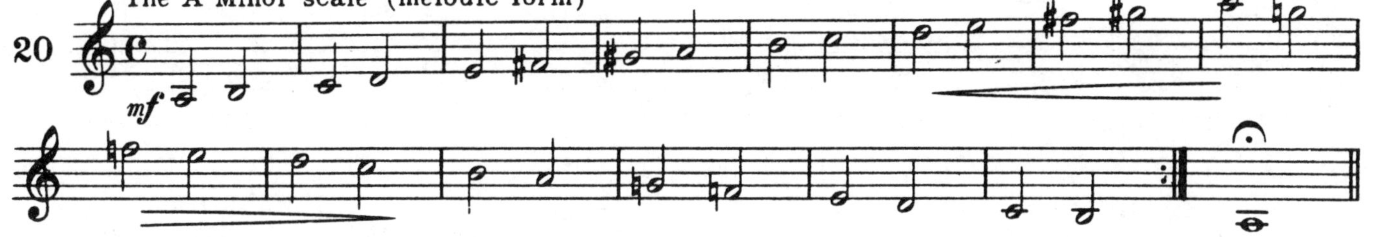

Note: The A Minor scale should also be practiced according to the patterns given on page 5

The A Minor chord (also play in quarters, 8ths, 16ths, — and slurred. See p. 5)

21

22

23

An Etude in A Minor

Allegro moderato

24

A Tone Study

25

Etude

26

A Staccato Exercise

27

The G Major scale

28 

Note: The G Major scale should also be practiced according to the patterns given on page 5

The G Major Chord (also play in quarters, 8ths, 16ths, and slurred)

29 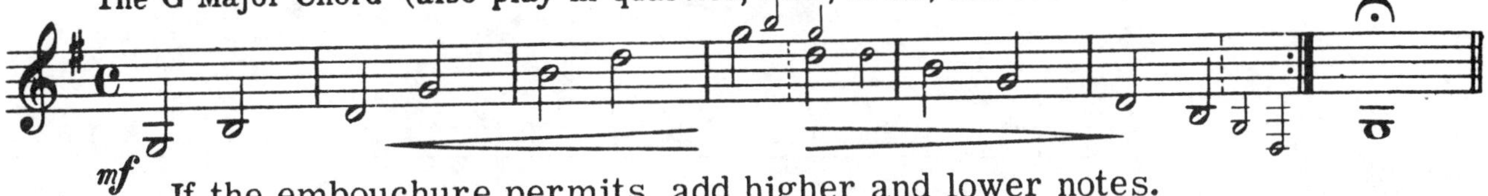

If the embouchure permits, add higher and lower notes.

30 

A suggestion to improve ones embouchure and range.

31 Play the "G" with a natural easy lip.

With the same lip start playing the following scale.

Continue in the same manner, always one half tone step higher, up to the C scale.

An Etude in G Major

Allegretto

32 

A Tone Study

A Staccato Exercise

*This mark (>) indicates a slight marcato, placed thus (∧), a more decisive marcato.

The E Minor scale (harmonic form) also practice according to the patterns on p. 5

35

The E Minor scale (melodic form) also play according to the patterns on p. 5

36

Note: The E Minor scale should also be practiced according to the patterns given on page 5

The E Minor chord (also play in quarters, 8ths, 16ths, and slurred)

37
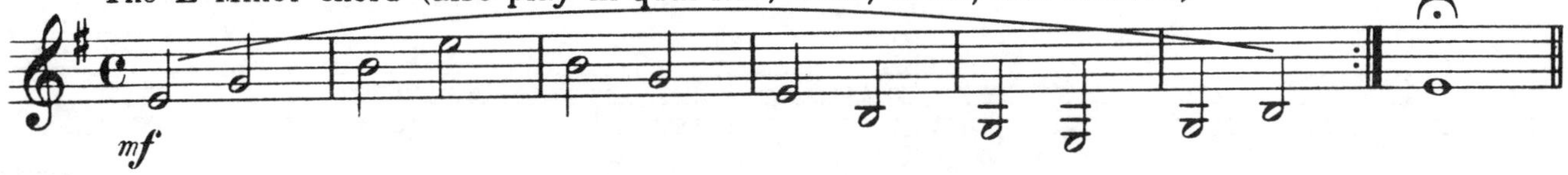

38

Arpeggio

39

An Etude in E Minor

Allegretto grazioso

40

A Tone Study

Etude

The F Major scale

43 

Note: The F Major scale should also be practiced according to the patterns given on page 5

The F Major chord (also play in quarters, 8ths, 16ths, and slurred)

44 

45 

46 

Chromatic

47 

An Etude in F Major

Moderato

48 

A Tone Study

Adagio

49

Etude

Allegretto scherzando (♩=76)

50

A Chord Exercise

Moderato

*see footnote

51

* The symbol indicates that the *two* preceding measures are to be repeated.

The D Minor scale (harmonic form) also play according to patterns on p. 5

52

The D Minor scale (melodic form) also play according to patterns on p. 5

53
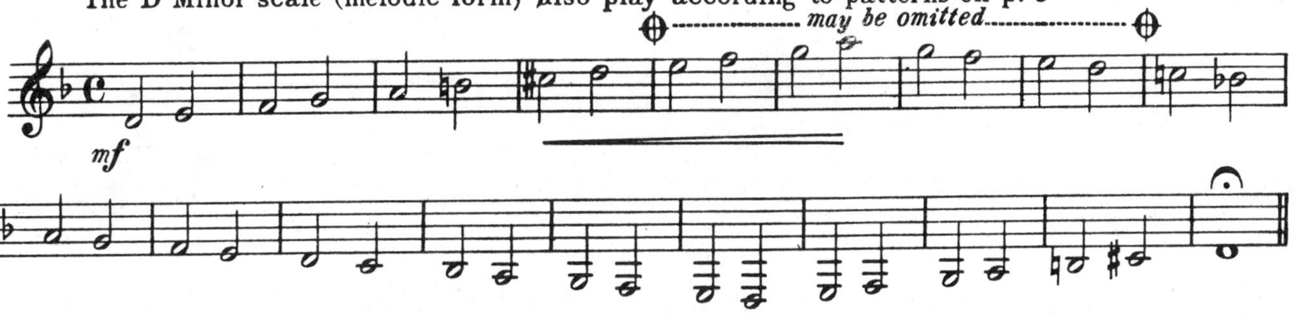

The D Minor chord (also play in quarters, 8ths, 16ths, and slurred)

54

55

56

An Etude in D Minor

57

A Tone Study

A Scale Exercise

60

Note: The D Major scale should also be practiced according to the patterns given on page 5

61
62
63
64

An Etude in D Major

65

A Tone Study

Adagio – for tone Production

66

Moderato

67

Moderato

68

The B Minor scale (harmonic form) also practice according to patterns on page 5

69
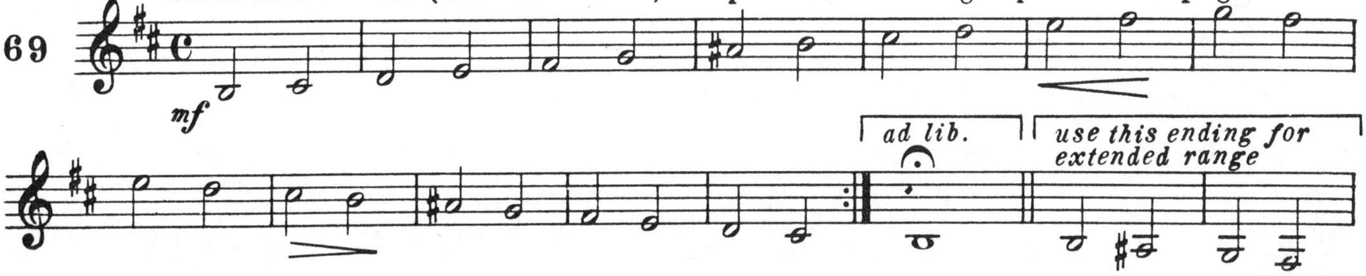

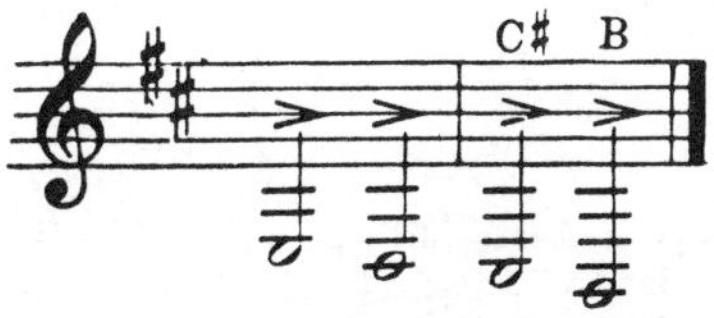

(The low notes of the last two measures are often written in the Bass Clef: In this book, all Bass Cleff examples are written according to the modern system of notation.)

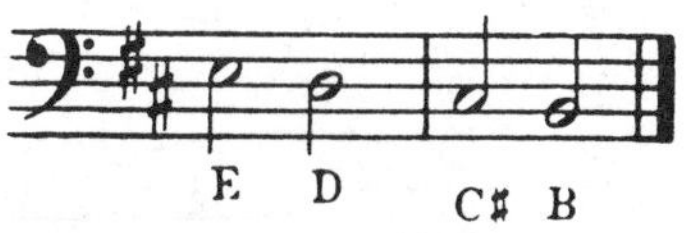

The B Minor scale (melodic form) also practice according to patterns on page 5

70
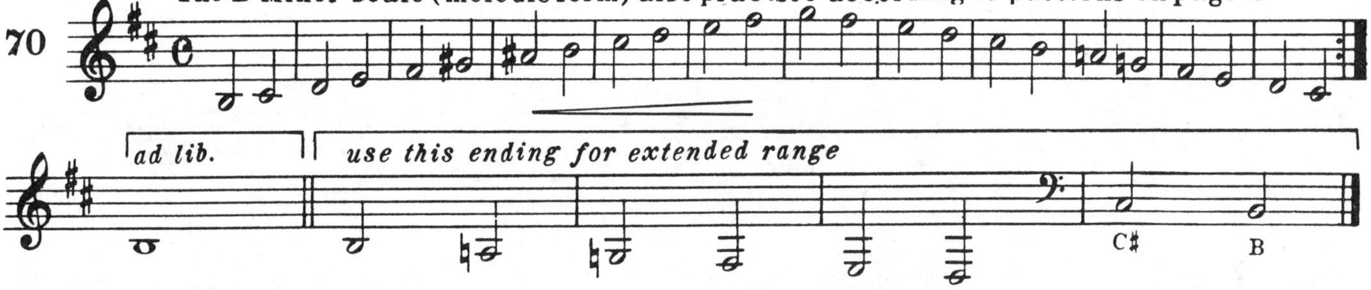

The B Minor chord (also played in quarters, eights, sixteenths,- and slurred. See page 5)

71
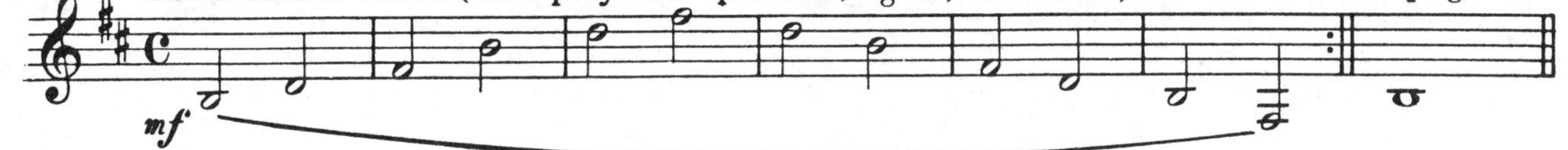

72

An Etude in B Minor

Andante

73

Adagio-very slow
74
pp
Allegretto
75
p
mf
f
p
p
Moderato
76
p a clean staccato
mf
p
mf
f
mf
f

An Etude in B♭ Major

A Tone Study

Very slowly, with full and dark tonequality
82
mf
f
f
Maestoso
83
f marcato
mf
f
mf
ff
Slowly at first - increase speed
84
mf
85
mf staccato
This exercise should also be practiced - (slurred)

An Etude in G Minor

*A – (dash) indicates that the note should be held full value, still some composers, Rachmaninoff for instance, calls for a slight marcato by such marking.

Adagio

92

Allegretto

93

Moderato - later Allegro

94

The A Major scale

95

The A Major chord

96

97

98

Chromatic - also practice slurred.

99

An Etude in A Major

Maestoso

100

A Tone Study

*As the · (dot) indicates a shorter note, about half of its value, the ʌ (wedge) calls for a still shorter (almost hammered) one, according to the character of the composition.

The F♯ Minor scale (harmonic form)

105 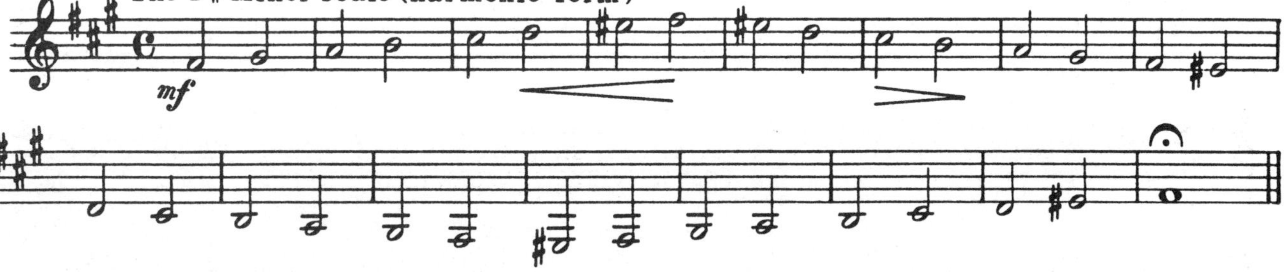

The F♯ Minor scale (melodic form)

106 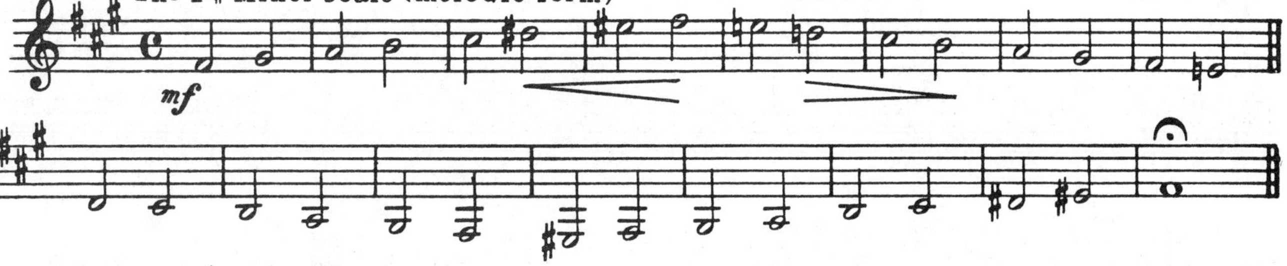

The F♯ Minor chord

107 

108 

109 

An Etude in F♯ Minor

Allegro moderato

110 

111
Adagio
p
f
p
f
f
p
mf
f
mf
rall.
112
Allegretto-gracioso
p
f
p
cresc.
f
113
Moderato
mf
Fine
mf
f
mf
f
rit.
D.C.

114

115

116

117

118

An Etude in E♭ Major

119

A Tone Study

Adagio
120
mf
f
Andante
121
p
rall.
staccato – play slowly at first, with a clean attack.
122
+ Cut .... +

The C Minor scale (harmonic form)

123

The C Minor scale (melodic form)

124

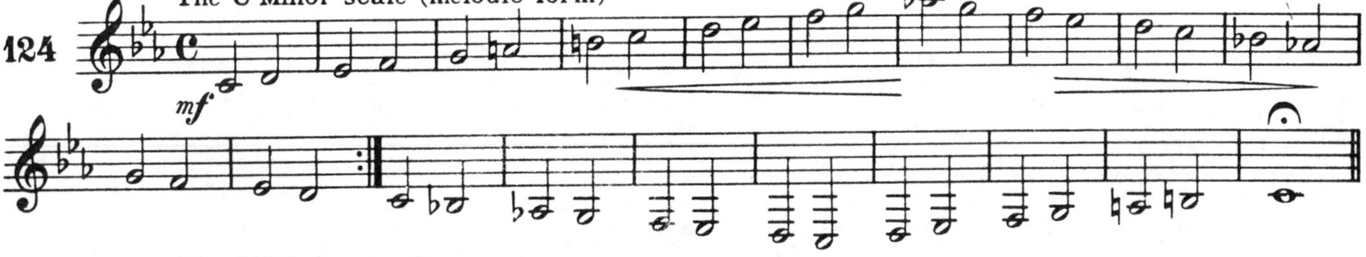

The C Minor chord

125

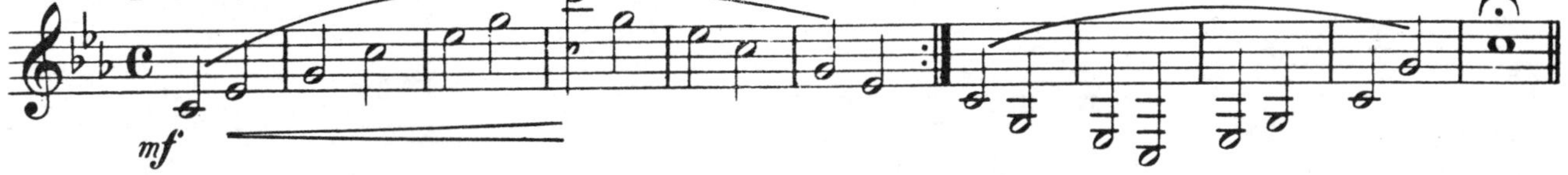

126

127

An Etude in C Minor

Allegro moderato

128

A Tone Study

Adagio molto
129
p
mf
p
mf
f
f
mf
a little faster
f
mf
very slow
f
Moderato
130
p
mf
cresc.
f
p
mf
f
ff

An Etude in E Major

Adagio (very slow) – in 8th
137
p
mf
f
mf
Con moto
cresc.
f
Tempo I
p
mf
f
rit.
Moderato–con grazia
138
p
p
mf
f
p
mf
cresc.
f

The C♯ Minor scale (harmonic form)

139 

The C♯ Minor scale (melodic form)

140 

The C♯ Minor Chord

141 

142 

143 

An Etude in C♯ Minor

Maestoso

144 

Andante con moto – In the deep cellar
FISCHER
145
f
mf
f
f
rit.
Allegro – lightly
146
p
f
mf
always staccato
mf
p
mf
f
Moderato
147
mf
2nd Ending
Fine
1st Ending
rit.
p
f
D.C.

The A♭ Major scale

148

The A♭ Major chord

149

150

151

Chromatic–also practice slurred

152

An Etude in A♭ Major

Andante

153

Maestoso
154
f
mf
p
mf cresc.
Moderato-Play lightly
155
p
Moderato
156
mf
f

The F Minor scale (harmonic form)

The F Minor scale (melodic form)

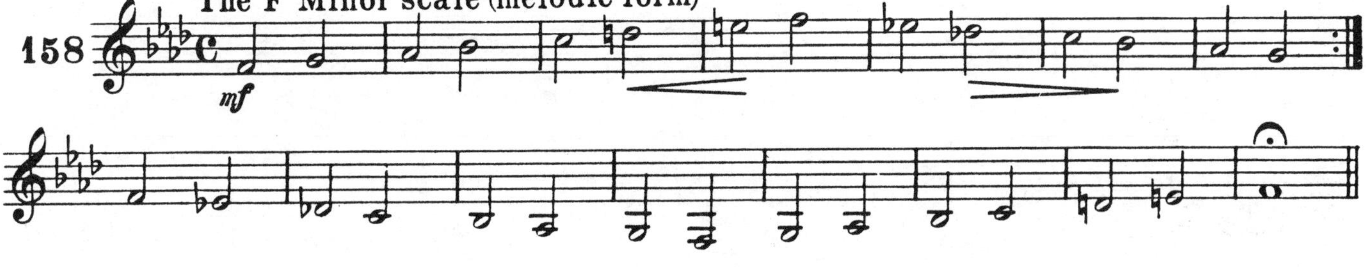

The F Minor chord

An Etude in F Minor

Adagio - in 8th
163
Slowly-with perfect attack
164
mf cresc.
ad lib
simile-cresc.
ad lib

Chords of the Dominant Seventh

165 166 167 168 169 170 171

Chords of the Diminished Seventh

172 173 174 175 176 177 178

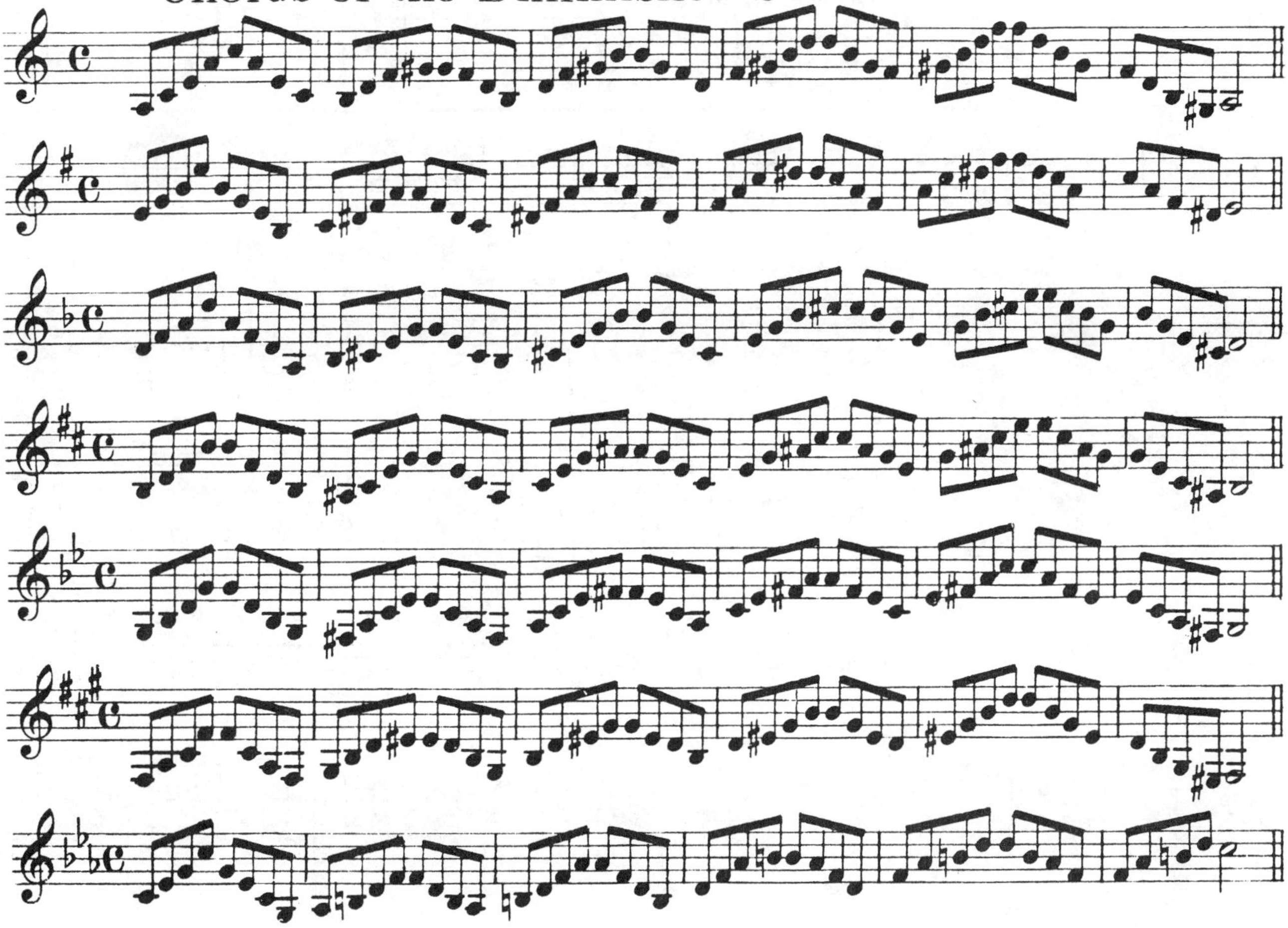

Andante
179
mf
f
mf
f
p
mf
p
mf
f
Moderato
180
p
p
f
p
f
p
f
f
rit.
181
p
simile

Embellishments

Embellishments have the purpose of enchancing or intensifying a simple note, to add grace to a singing but otherwise simple line of melody, or to imply humor, elegance, or capriciousness. They are divided into two groups:

A. Those which are written out in small print, including:
1. The short grace note or Acciaccatura
2. The long grace note or Appoggiature
3. Two or more grace notes

B. Those which are implied and which are indicated by signs, including:
1. The Trill
2. The Shake or Mordent
3. The Turn or Grupetto

The Short Grace Note (Acciaccatura)

A dash through the stem of a grace note indentifies it as the short variety. It derives its value from the preceding beat and is light, unaccented, and usually slurred to the following principal note.

written:
182
played:

The Long Grace Note (Appoggiatura)

The long grace note has no dash through its stem. Contrary to the short grace note, it is played on the beat. Its duration is generally half the time value of the following principal note, but when the appoggiatura precedes a dotted note it receives two-thirds the time value of the principal note.

written:
183
played:

Two Or More Grace Notes

These should take their time value from the preceding beat as given below. If they are to be ON the beat, they must be written out as intended

written:
184
played:

The Trill

The trill is a rapid repetition of two consecutive notes. It starts on the written note and is followed by the next higher one. Both notes are governed by the key signature unless an accidental accompanies the trill sign in which case the accidental affects the higher of the two notes.

written:
185
played:

The Shake (Mordent)

The Shake is indicated by the sign (𝆗) [It consists of the principal note and the note above. Both notes are governed by the key signature unless the sign is accompanied by an accidental. The inverted Mordent (𝆘) should also be mentioned. In this case, the auxiliary tone is below the principal note.

written:
186
played:

written:
187
played:

The Turn (Gruppetto)

The Turn (∞) is a symbol for FOUR ADDED NOTES. They are, in order, as follows: (1) The note above the principal note, (2) The principal note, (3) The note below the principal note, (4) The principal note. Identify them in the example given.

written:
188
played:

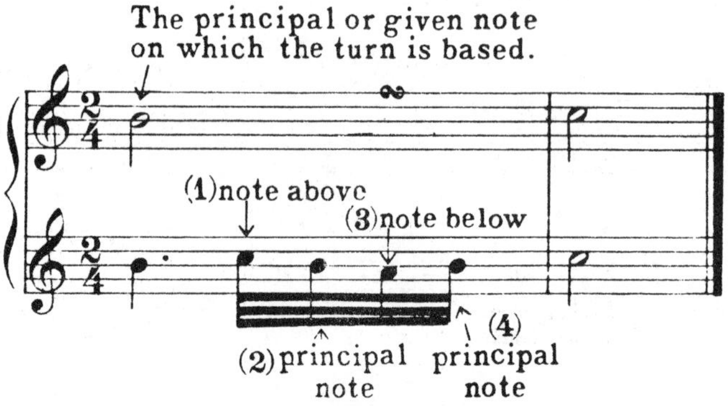

∾ indicates turn from above

∾ indicates turn from below

The Turn *(Continued)*

It will be noted in the examples below that all notes of the turn are governed by the key signature unless an accidental accompanies the turn sign. If the accidental is <u>above</u> the sign, the highest note is affected; if the accidental is <u>below</u> the sign, the lowest note of the turn is affected.

The rhythm of the turn (values of the added notes) is determined largely by the tempo of the composition being played, and to some extent by the style, but it will be seen in the examples given that the performer can depend on one of two traditional interpretations. It may be said, however, that regardless of the tempo, EVERY NOTE SHOULD SOUND, and that a "blurry" effect must always be avoided.

189

written:

played:

190

written:

played:

also played:

191

written:

played:

also played:

192 written: / played: / also played:

193 written / played:

194 written / played:

The turn is sometimes reversed, with the lower note being played first.
The example is from Overture to "Rienzi" by Richard Wagner.

Horn in F
195

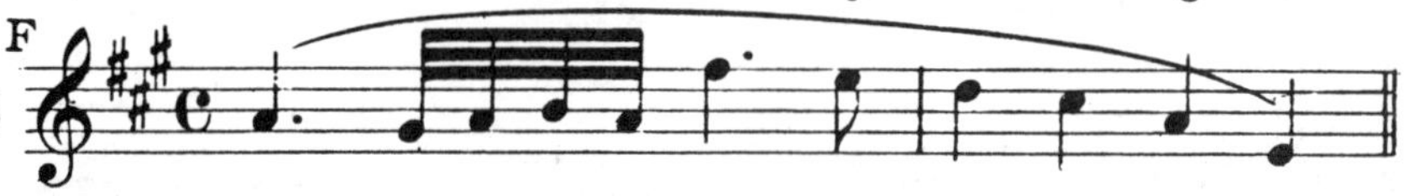

Few modern composers designate whether the turn shall start above or below the principal note, although this is sometimes done by writing out the turn in full. Tradition, of course, dictates the method in the older compositions.

196

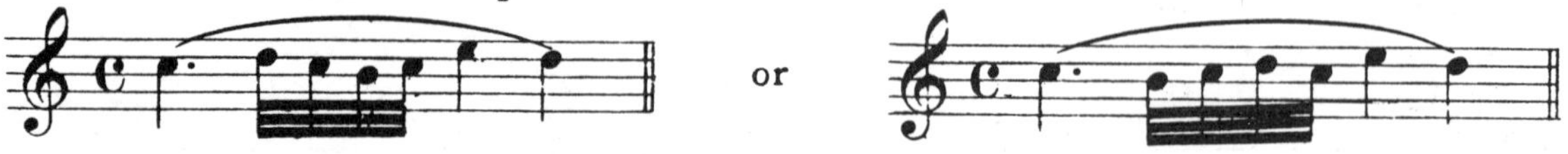

The turn <u>above</u> a note. It consists either of a higher note, principal note and longer note, or of the lower note, principal note and higher note. <u>The first turn</u> note is <u>on</u> the beat.

197 written / played:

Adagio
198
Andante
199
Adagio
200

Duet

See the Conquering Hero Comes

HÄNDEL

Moderato

201

Trio

Nocturno from "Midsummer Nights Dream"

Mendelssohn

Andante con moto

202